People of the Bible

The Bible through stories and pictures

Miracles by the Sea

Copyright © in this format Belitha Press Ltd., 1983

Text copyright © Catherine Storr 1983

Illustrations copyright © Chris Molan 1983

Art Director: Treld Bicknell

First published in the United States of America 1983
by Raintree Publishers Inc.
310 West Wisconsin Avenue, Milwaukee, Wisconsin 53203
in association with Belitha Press Ltd., London.

Conceived, designed and produced by Belitha Press Ltd.,
2 Beresford Terrace, London N5 2DH

ISBN 0-8172-1983-8 (U.S.A.)

Library of Congress Cataloging in Publication Data

Storr, Catherine.
    Miracles by the sea.

    (People of the Bible)
    Summary: A simple retelling of the New Testament
accounts of miracles performed by Jesus Christ.
    1. Jesus—Miracles—Juvenile literature. [1. Jesus
Christ—Miracles. 2. Bible stories—N.T.] I. Molan,
Christine, ill. II. Title.
BT366.S76   1983   226'.709505   82-23022

ISBN 0-8172-1983-8

Printed in The United States of America.

  567891011121314 97 96 95 94 93 92 91 90 89 88

Miracles
by the Sea

Retold by Catherine Storr

Pictures by Chris Molan

Raintree Childrens Books
Milwaukee
Belitha Press Limited • London

One day Jesus was preaching on the shore. A great crowd of people came to hear him. He saw two boats in the water nearby. One of them belonged to Simon. Jesus got into it and asked Simon to push out a little into the lake. Then he sat down and talked to the people from the boat.

Afterward Jesus said to Simon, "Take the boat out into the deep water, and let down the net so that you can catch some fish."

"Master, I'll do what you tell me," said Simon, "but we've been fishing all night, and we haven't caught a single one."

Simon went out with his boat into the middle of the lake and let down the net. So many fish swam into it, it broke when Simon tried to pull it in. There were enough fish to fill two boats.

Another day, Jesus was in the desert. A great many people came to listen to his teachings.

Some of them asked him to make them well. Jesus was sorry for them, and he healed many of the sick people.

When it was evening, Jesus' disciples said to him, "Send all these people away. It is late, and they should go and buy food."

"Some of them have been here for three days without eating," Jesus said. "If we send them away now, they will faint on the way."

"Have we got any food for them here?"
Jesus asked.

The disciples said, "There's a lad here
with five loaves of bread and two fish.
That's not nearly enough."

Jesus said to them, "Bring the bread and fish here. Tell all the people to sit down in groups of fifty." Then he blessed the five loaves and the two fish and began to hand them out to the people, who ate as much as they wanted. Even so, there was enough left over to fill twelve baskets.

Afterward Jesus sent the people away. He wanted to be alone. He went into the mountains by himself.

His disciples boarded a ship and began to sail over the sea toward Capernaum. Suddenly a great wind began to blow and the sea became rough, with huge, frightening waves.

The disciples were a long way from land and in great danger. Then they saw someone walking toward them on top of the rough seas. They were terrified, and thought it was a ghost.

"Don't be frightened," Jesus shouted. "It's only me."

"If it's really you, Master," said Peter, "tell me to walk on the water, too."

"All right, then, walk toward me," said Jesus.

Peter got out of the ship and started walking on the water toward Jesus. But the wind blew hard, and he was frightened. He couldn't stay on top of the water and began to sink.

"Lord, save me," Peter called out.

Jesus put out his hand and caught Peter. "You didn't have enough faith," he said, "Why did you begin to doubt? You could have gone on."

When they got back onto the ship, the wind stopped blowing, and they were safe.

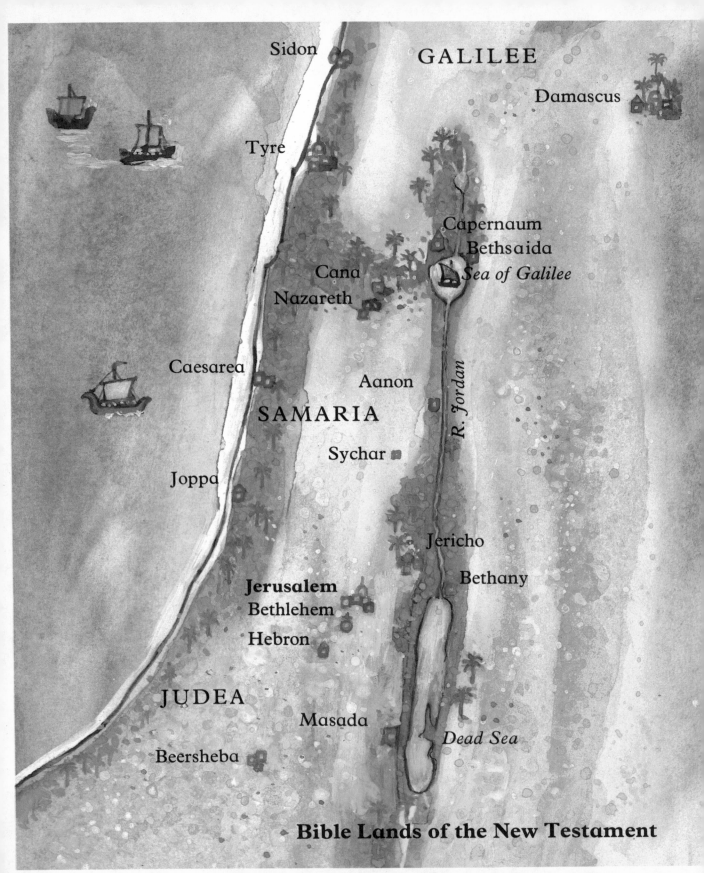

Sidon

GALILEE

Damascus

Tyre

Capernaum

Bethsaida

Cana

Sea of Galilee

Nazareth

Caesarea

Aanon

R. Jordan

SAMARIA

Sychar

Joppa

Jericho

Bethany

Jerusalem

Bethlehem

Hebron

JUDEA

Masada

Dead Sea

Beersheba

Bible Lands of the New Testament